W9-AXK-110

Materials, Materials, Materials

Paper

Chris Oxlade

Heinemann Library
Chicago, Illinois

Designed by Storeybooks
Originated by Ambassador Litho Ltd.
Printed in Hong Kong / China

05 04 03 02 01
10 9 8 7 6 5 4 3 2 1

Library of Congress Cataloging-in-Publication Data

Oxlade, Chris.
  Paper / by Chris Oxlade.
      p. cm. -- (Materials, materials, materials)
Includes bibliographical references and index.
  ISBN 1-58810-156-8
  1. Paper--Juvenile literature. 2. Papermaking--Juvenile literature.
[1. Paper.] I. Title. II. Series.
  TS1105.5 .O95 2001
  676--dc21

                               00-012892

Acknowledgments

The author and publishers are grateful to the following for permission to reproduce copyright material:
Corbis/Philip Gould, p. 4; Tudor Photography, pp. 5, 6, 7, 8, 9, 10, 22; Powerstock Zefa, pp. 11, 16, 28; Science Photo Library/Microfield Scientific Ltd., p. 12; Science Photo Library/Tommaso Guicciardini, p. 13; Corbis, p. 14; Science Photo Library/Colin Cuthbert, p. 15; Jacqui Hurst, p. 17; Corbis/RonWatts, p. 18; Photodisc, pp. 19, 20, 21, 27; Corbis/Jacqui Hurst, p. 23; DIY Photo Library, p. 24; Elizabeth Whiting Associates, p. 25; Corbis/Paul Seheult/Eye Ubiquitous, p. 26.

Every effort has been made to contact copyright holders of any material reproduced in this book.
Any omissions will be rectified in subsequent printings if notice is given to the publisher.

Note to the Reader
Some words are shown in bold, **like this.**
You can find out what they mean by looking in the glossary.

gft
3-14-05

Contents

What Is Paper?

Paper is made in workshops and **factories.** It is not a **natural** material. This paper has just been made. It is ready to be made into newspapers.

Paper has many uses. It can be used to
make lots of different things. All the things
in this picture are made of paper.

Strong and Weak

Paper is easy to tear into pieces. It is also easy to scrunch up into a ball. A sheet of paper is very strong, though, if you try to stretch it or pull it apart.

A sheet of paper can be made stronger by folding it. The fan in this picture is stiff because of the folds in the paper.

Paper and Cardboard

There are many different kinds of paper.
Sometimes paper is colored with **dyes.**
The paper in this book has a smooth,
shiny **surface.** Other types of paper
feel rough when you touch them.

Cardboard is made from paper. It is very thick and stiff. It often has a wavy sheet of thick, stiff paper between two flat pieces. This makes the cardboard stronger than regular paper.

Wet and Dry

Paper towels and napkins are very
absorbent. Water flows into tiny spaces
inside the paper. If it gets too wet, the
paper will fall apart.

Cups for holding **liquids** are sometimes made from paper. The paper is covered with a thin layer of **wax** or plastic. This makes the paper **waterproof.**

Making Paper

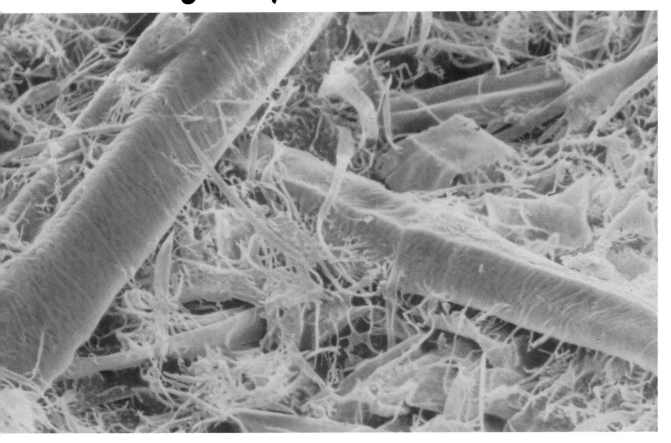

Paper is made from tiny **fibers.** You can see the fibers when you tear paper. Most paper fibers come from wood. The wood comes from trees.

Paper is made at a **factory** called a **paper mill.** Wood is mixed with water and **chemicals.** Then it is mashed into a thick paste called wood **pulp.**

Drying and Rolling

The runny wood **pulp** is poured onto a wire mesh. The mesh catches the wood **fibers** but lets the water drain away. This makes a layer of wet paper.

Then the paper is taken off of the mesh. The rest of the water is squeezed out of it with heavy rollers. The paper is dried and put on big rolls or cut into sheets.

Writing and Painting

Paper for writing has a smooth **surface.**
It is coated with **chemicals.** They stop
ink from soaking into the paper too
much and smearing.

This painting is being done on thick, **absorbent** paper. It is called watercolor paper. It soaks up the watery paint. Then it dries out when the painting is finished.

Printing on Paper

Most paper is made into newspapers, books, and magazines. In this picture, a large roll of paper is going through a newspaper **press.**

Paper money is printed on paper that has strong **fibers** in it. This makes the paper hard to tear. Most money lasts more than a year before it wears out.

Paper Packaging

Many packaging materials are made from paper. Paper bags are made by folding and gluing thick paper.

Cardboard is used to make strong boxes. Here, flat pieces of cardboard are being stacked in a **factory.** Each one can be folded to make a box. The edges of a box are joined with tape, glue, or **staples.**

Things Made from Paper

Many objects are made by cutting, folding, and gluing paper. The boxes and airplanes in this picture are made of paper.

The plate in this picture is made of a material called **papier mâché.** You make papier mâché by using wet paper and glue. It becomes hard when it dries.

Paper in Homes

The walls of this home are being covered with wallpaper. The wallpaper is thick and heavy. The man is using glue to put it on the walls.

In some Japanese-style homes, screens are used between rooms instead of walls. Sheets of paper are glued onto wooden frames to make the screens and sliding doors.

Recycling Paper

Millions of trees are cut down every day to make paper. **Paper mills** use lots of electricity to make paper. We can save trees and electricity by **recycling** paper.

Paper that is sent to be recycled is smashed into wood **pulp.** Any ink or **dye** on it is taken off with **chemicals.** Most recycled paper is used to make newspapers and **cardboard.**

Please Recycle

Fact File

▶ Most paper is made in **factories.** It is not a **natural** material.

▶ Paper is easy to scrunch up and to tear.

▶ Paper is hard to stretch and pull apart.

▶ Paper can be made stiffer by folding it.

▶ Paper can be smooth or rough. It can be white or colored.

▶ **Cardboard** is thicker than regular paper.

▶ Paper is **absorbent.** It also can be made to be **waterproof.**

▶ Paper does not let electricity or heat flow through it.

▶ Paper burns when it is heated.

▶ Paper is not attracted by **magnets.**

▶ Paper can be **recycled.**

Can You Believe It?

A roll of paper can be as tall as an adult person and as heavy as a car! If you unrolled a newspaper roll, it would be about nine miles (fifteen kilometers) long. It would take an adult three hours to walk that far!

Glossary

absorbent soaks up water easily

cardboard very stiff material made from layers of thick paper

chemical material used to clean or protect something

dye chemical used to color something

factory place where things are made using machines

fiber very thin thread or small piece of material as thin as one of your hairs

liquid something that flows, such as water or oil

magnet piece of iron or steel that pulls iron or steel things toward it

natural comes from plants, animals, or rocks in the earth

papier mâché material made from mixing paper and glue

paper mill factory where paper is made

press machine that prints ink onto paper

pulp mixture of wood and water that has been mashed together

recycle to use a material again, often to make new things

staple thin piece of metal that sticks through sheets of paper or cardboard to hold them together

surface top or outside of an object

waterproof does not let water in or out

wax material that feels smooth and oily and does not let water through

More Books to Read

Broutzas, Sharon. *Paper Crafts.* Lake Forest, Ill.: Forest House Publishing, 1998.

Madgwick, Wendy. *Super Materials.* Austin, Tex.: Raintree Steck-Vaughn, 1999.

Gibbons, Gail. *Recycle!: A Handbook for Kids.* New York: Little, Brown & Co., 1996.

Index